To My Father and Mentor
Daryl P. Kelly

Introduction

In an age where digital connectivity and information exchange are at the heart of virtually every aspect of our lives, the role of System and Network Administration has taken center stage. From the bustling data centers that power global businesses to the cozy home networks that keep us connected, these unsung heroes of the digital realm ensure that the complex machinery of modern technology hums along seamlessly. This book, "Mastering System and Network Administration: A Comprehensive Guide to Effective IT Management," is your essential companion on a journey to becoming a proficient and successful administrator of IT systems and networks.

The Role and Importance of System and Network Administration

Imagine a world without the wizards who monitor, configure, secure, and troubleshoot the intricate systems that underpin our digital interactions. System and network administrators are the architects and custodians of the digital landscapes we traverse daily. They are the guardians of data integrity, the gatekeepers of network security, and the responders to the inevitable hiccups that arise in even the most finely-tuned infrastructures. This book seeks to equip you with the knowledge, skills, and mindset required to excel in these roles.

Evolving Landscape of IT Infrastructure

As technology advances at an astonishing pace, the IT landscape continuously evolves. Cloud computing, virtualization, containerization, IoT devices, and AI-driven automation are reshaping the way we conceptualize and manage IT environments. In the face of such transformations, the foundational principles of system and network administration remain steadfast while adapting to new paradigms. This book embraces this dynamic landscape, providing you with insights into both the timeless principles and the cutting-edge techniques that are essential to stay ahead in this field.

Whether you are a budding IT enthusiast looking to embark on a rewarding career or a seasoned professional seeking to refine your expertise, "Mastering System and Network Administration" is designed to be your compass, guiding you through the complexities of administering systems and networks with confidence. Each chapter of this book is crafted to provide a clear understanding of the fundamental concepts, practical insights, and hands-on skills necessary to excel in the world of IT administration.

So, buckle up and prepare to delve into the realms of operating systems, networking essentials, security best practices, automation, troubleshooting, and more. As you navigate through these pages, remember that mastering system and network administration is not just about managing technology—it's about enabling and enhancing the digital experiences of individuals, businesses, and societies at large. Your journey starts here.

1

UNDERSTANDING SYSTEM ADMINISTRATION

In the ever-evolving landscape of technology, where the digital realm interweaves seamlessly with our daily lives, the role of a system administrator stands as a critical pillar of support. System administrators, often referred to as sysadmins, are the architects of the digital infrastructure that powers organizations, connects communities, and drives innovation. In this chapter, we'll dive into the core concepts of system administration, exploring its definition, scope, key responsibilities, and the essential qualities that set exceptional sysadmins apart.

Definition and Scope of System Administration

At its core, system administration is the practice of managing and maintaining the hardware, software, and network resources that make up an information system. These systems range from individual computers to complex networks, data centers, and cloud environments. The role encompasses a wide spectrum of tasks, including system setup, configuration, monitoring, security, troubleshooting, and performance optimization.

System administrators are responsible for creating an environment where technology seamlessly serves the needs of users, applications, and the organization as a whole. They ensure the availability, reliability, and scalability of IT resources, enabling businesses to operate efficiently and individuals to interact with technology without hindrance.

Key Responsibilities and Roles

The responsibilities of a system administrator can vary depending on the size and complexity of the infrastructure they manage. Some common responsibilities include:

1. **Installation and Configuration:** Sysadmins set up new systems, install operating systems and software, and configure them to meet specific requirements. This involves fine-tuning settings, creating user accounts, and establishing network connections.

2. **Security:** Securing systems and data is a paramount concern. Sysadmins implement security measures such as firewalls, encryption, access controls, and regular security updates to protect against threats and breaches.

3. **Monitoring and Maintenance:** System administrators continuously monitor the health and performance of systems, responding to alerts and proactively addressing potential issues. Regular maintenance tasks like updates, patches, and backups are essential to prevent downtime and data loss.

4. **Troubleshooting:** When problems arise, sysadmins use their expertise to diagnose and resolve issues. This requires a

deep understanding of system components, networking protocols, and troubleshooting methodologies.

5. **Performance Optimization:** Ensuring optimal performance involves monitoring resource usage, identifying bottlenecks, and implementing enhancements to improve efficiency.

6. **Documentation:** Maintaining thorough documentation of system configurations, processes, and procedures is crucial for knowledge sharing, troubleshooting, and disaster recovery.

Skills and Qualities of a Successful System Administrator

Becoming an effective system administrator requires a blend of technical skills, interpersonal qualities, and a problem-solving mindset. Some essential skills and qualities include:

- **Technical Proficiency:** A solid foundation in operating systems, networking, scripting, and security is vital. Familiarity with multiple platforms and technologies enhances versatility.
- **Attention to Detail:** System administrators must be meticulous, ensuring that configurations are accurate, security measures are in place, and potential issues are addressed before they escalate.
- **Adaptability:** The IT landscape evolves rapidly. Sysadmins need to stay current with emerging technologies and trends to adapt their strategies and approaches.
- **Communication Skills:** Effective communication is essential when working with colleagues, end-users, and stakeholders. Explaining technical concepts in accessible language fosters collaboration.
- **Problem-Solving:** System administrators are perpetual problem solvers. They approach challenges methodically, utilizing diagnostic tools and their own analytical abilities.

- **Time Management:** Juggling multiple tasks and priorities requires strong time management skills to maintain system stability and address urgent matters promptly.

In the world of system administration, your role is akin to being the invisible hand that keeps the gears of technology turning smoothly. From ensuring that an organization's email server runs without a glitch to safeguarding critical databases, the responsibilities of a sysadmin are as diverse as they are impactful. As you progress through this book, remember that mastering system administration isn't just about managing systems—it's about empowering the digital infrastructure that powers the modern world.

2
OPERATING SYSTEMS ESSENTIALS

Operating systems serve as the foundation upon which all computing activities rest. They are the interface between hardware and software, enabling users and applications to interact with computer resources efficiently. In this chapter, we'll explore the fundamentals of operating systems, their types, installation procedures, configuration nuances, and the vital role they play in the realm of system administration.

Introduction to Different Operating Systems

Operating systems come in various flavors, each tailored to specific use cases and environments. Some of the most common operating systems include:

- **Windows:** Microsoft's Windows operating system is widely used in both personal and enterprise environments. It offers a user-friendly interface, compatibility with a wide range of applications, and extensive administrative tools.
- **Linux:** Linux is an open-source operating system that comes in numerous distributions (distros). It's renowned for its

stability, security, and flexibility. Linux is prevalent in server environments and is often the choice for web hosting, cloud computing, and embedded systems.

- **macOS:** Developed by Apple, macOS powers Apple's line of computers. It's known for its sleek design, integration with Apple hardware and software, and robust multimedia capabilities.
- **Unix:** Unix laid the groundwork for many modern operating systems, including Linux and macOS. It's renowned for its multitasking and multiuser capabilities, making it a staple in server environments.

Installation, Configuration, and Maintenance

Installing an operating system involves preparing the system hardware, booting from installation media (such as a DVD or USB drive), and following prompts to configure settings. This process can vary based on the operating system and the hardware it's being installed on.

Configuration involves tailoring the operating system to meet specific needs. This includes setting up network connections, user accounts, security settings, and software installations. Configuration files and administrative tools play a crucial role in this process.

Maintenance is an ongoing effort to keep the operating system running smoothly. This includes applying updates and patches to address security vulnerabilities and improve performance. Regular maintenance tasks help prevent system instability and security breaches.

Command-Line Interface (CLI) Basics

The command-line interface (CLI) is a powerful tool for system administrators. It provides direct access to the operating system through text-based commands. Common CLI tasks include navigating the file system, managing files and directories, running scripts, and configuring system settings. Familiarity with the CLI is essential for efficient system administration, as it allows administrators to perform tasks quickly and automate repetitive processes.

In the realm of system administration, operating systems are the canvases upon which administrators paint their masterpieces. Each stroke of configuration, each command executed, and each update applied contributes to the stability, security, and functionality of the IT landscape. Understanding the nuances of different operating systems, their installation procedures, and the power of the command line sets the stage for your journey as a proficient system administrator. As you delve into the complexities of this chapter, remember that a strong foundation in operating systems is key to mastering the art of system administration.

3

NETWORKING FUNDAMENTALS

In the digital age, where global connectivity is the norm, understanding the fundamentals of networking is essential for every system administrator. Networks are the highways along which data flows, enabling communication, collaboration, and resource sharing. This chapter delves into the core concepts of networking, from the fundamental protocols that power the internet to the architecture of local and wide-area networks.

TCP/IP Protocol Suite

At the heart of modern networking is the TCP/IP protocol suite. This collection of protocols governs the way data is exchanged across networks, including the internet. The suite comprises two main protocols:

- **Transmission Control Protocol (TCP):** TCP ensures reliable data delivery by breaking down messages into packets, sending them, and verifying their receipt. It manages the establishment and termination of connections, as well as flow control to prevent overwhelming a recipient.

- **Internet Protocol (IP):** IP is responsible for routing packets of data from source to destination across interconnected networks. It assigns unique IP addresses to devices and uses these addresses to determine the most efficient path for data transmission.

Network Topologies and Components

Networks are structured in various topologies, each defining how devices are interconnected. Common topologies include:

- **Star Topology:** Devices are connected to a central hub or switch.
- **Bus Topology:** Devices are connected along a central cable or backbone.
- **Ring Topology:** Devices are connected in a circular chain.
- **Mesh Topology:** Devices are interconnected with multiple direct connections.

Network components include routers, switches, hubs, and access points. Routers facilitate data exchange between different networks, switches manage data traffic within a network, hubs connect devices in a network, and access points provide wireless connectivity.

IP Addressing and Subnetting

IP addresses are essential for identifying devices on a network. IPv4 addresses are composed of four sets of numbers separated by dots (e.g., 192.168.1.1). IPv6 addresses, designed to address the depletion of IPv4 addresses, are longer and more flexible.

Subnetting involves dividing a larger network into smaller

subnetworks, or subnets. This practice improves efficiency by limiting broadcast traffic and aiding in network management.

DNS and DHCP Concepts

The Domain Name System (DNS) translates human-readable domain names (e.g., www.example.com) into IP addresses. This translation is crucial for browsing the internet and accessing resources.

Dynamic Host Configuration Protocol (DHCP) automates the assignment of IP addresses to devices in a network. It ensures efficient IP allocation and minimizes manual configuration.

Understanding networking fundamentals is like deciphering the intricate web that connects the digital world. From the way data packets traverse networks to the mechanisms that ensure seamless communication, networking concepts are at the core of effective system administration. As you journey through this chapter, remember that a solid grasp of networking is your passport to building and maintaining robust, interconnected systems that power modern organizations and drive global connectivity.

4
Network Infrastructure Setup and Management

A well-designed and efficiently managed network infrastructure is the backbone of modern organizations. From small businesses to large enterprises, the architecture and components of a network play a pivotal role in determining the reliability, scalability, and security of digital operations. In this chapter, we'll explore the intricacies of setting up and managing network infrastructures, including design considerations, network devices, and strategies for optimizing performance and security.

Designing and Planning Networks

The foundation of a robust network is laid during the design and planning phase. Considerations include:

- **Topology:** Selecting the appropriate network topology (star, bus, ring, mesh) based on the organization's needs and scalability requirements.

- **Scalability:** Anticipating growth and ensuring that the network can accommodate increased traffic and additional devices without significant disruptions.
- **Redundancy:** Implementing redundancy through backup links, devices, and paths to ensure network availability even in the face of failures.
- **Segmentation:** Dividing the network into segments or virtual LANs (VLANs) to improve performance and security by isolating traffic.

Network Devices (Routers, Switches, Firewalls, etc.)

Network devices play distinct roles in ensuring efficient data transmission, security, and control. Key devices include:

- **Routers:** Responsible for forwarding data between different networks, routers use routing tables to determine the best path for data packets.
- **Switches:** Switches manage data traffic within a network by forwarding data only to the device it's intended for, reducing congestion.
- **Firewalls:** Firewalls enforce security policies by filtering incoming and outgoing network traffic based on defined rules. They protect networks from unauthorized access and potential threats.
- **Load Balancers:** Load balancers distribute network traffic across multiple servers to ensure optimal resource utilization and prevent server overload.

Virtual LANs (VLANs) and Subnet Design

VLANs enable the segmentation of a network into isolated logical segments. Benefits include enhanced security, improved network performance, and simplified management.

Effective subnet design involves dividing IP address ranges into smaller subnets, optimizing resource utilization and network efficiency.

Network Security and Monitoring

Securing a network infrastructure is paramount to safeguarding sensitive data and ensuring uninterrupted operations. Key security measures include:

- **Access Control:** Implementing role-based access controls to restrict network access based on user roles and responsibilities.
- **Intrusion Detection and Prevention Systems (IDPS):** Deploying IDPS solutions to detect and mitigate unauthorized access attempts and potential threats.
- **Network Monitoring and Analysis Tools:** Employing monitoring tools to track network performance, identify anomalies, and troubleshoot issues in real-time.

Conclusion

Designing, implementing, and managing a robust network infrastructure requires a combination of strategic planning, technical expertise, and a commitment to security. As you explore the intricacies of network setup and management in this chapter, remember that a well-architected network is the foundation upon which all digital interactions and operations rely. Whether you're building a local office network or a global enterprise infrastructure, understanding the nuances of network devices, security measures, and best practices will empower you to create and maintain a resilient and high-performing network environment.

5
Network Security and Monitoring

In an era of pervasive digital interactions and global connectivity, network security is a paramount concern. Protecting sensitive data, ensuring the confidentiality of communications, and safeguarding against cyber threats are critical responsibilities of a system and network administrator. This chapter delves into the realm of network security and monitoring, exploring best practices, tools, and strategies to fortify network defenses and maintain a vigilant watch over the network landscape.

Network Security Best Practices

Network security is a multi-layered approach that involves a combination of strategies and technologies. Key best practices include:

- **Firewalls and Intrusion Prevention Systems (IPS):** Configuring firewalls to filter incoming and outgoing traffic based on defined rules, and implementing IPS to detect and prevent malicious activities.

- **Access Control:** Employing robust access control mechanisms to ensure that only authorized users and devices can access the network resources.
- **Encryption:** Using encryption protocols such as SSL/TLS to secure data transmissions and protect sensitive information from eavesdropping.
- **Patch Management:** Regularly applying security patches and updates to network devices and software to address known vulnerabilities.
- **Security Audits and Penetration Testing:** Conducting periodic security audits and penetration tests to identify vulnerabilities and weaknesses in the network infrastructure.

Intrusion Detection and Prevention Systems (IDPS)

IDPS are essential components of network security, serving as early warning systems against potential threats. They monitor network traffic for anomalies, unauthorized access attempts, and malicious activities. When abnormal behavior is detected, IDPS can take action to prevent or mitigate the threat, such as blocking suspicious IP addresses or generating alerts for further investigation.

Network Monitoring and Analysis Tools

Network monitoring tools are essential for maintaining a robust and secure network. These tools provide insights into network traffic, performance, and potential issues. Some key aspects of network monitoring include:

- **Traffic Analysis:** Monitoring network traffic patterns to detect abnormalities or signs of unauthorized access.
- **Performance Monitoring:** Tracking the performance of network devices and identifying potential bottlenecks or slowdowns.

- **Event Logging:** Logging network events and activities for auditing, troubleshooting, and security analysis.
- **Alerting and Notification:** Configuring alerts and notifications to promptly respond to critical network events and potential security breaches.

Security Incident Response

Despite the best preventive measures, security incidents may still occur. Having a well-defined incident response plan in place is crucial to minimizing damage and downtime. This plan should outline steps to take when a security incident is detected, including identifying the nature of the incident, containing its impact, eradicating the threat, and recovering normal operations.

Conclusion

Network security and monitoring form the bedrock of a resilient and trustworthy digital environment. As you navigate the complexities of this chapter, remember that the responsibility of a system and network administrator goes beyond mere management —it extends to safeguarding the integrity, confidentiality, and availability of critical data and services. By implementing rigorous security measures, employing advanced monitoring tools, and cultivating a proactive mindset, you empower your organization to face the ever-evolving landscape of cyber threats with confidence and resilience.

6
WIRELESS NETWORKING

Wireless networking has revolutionized the way we connect to information and interact with technology. From smartphones to smart homes and bustling corporate campuses, wireless networks provide the flexibility and mobility that modern lifestyles demand. This chapter explores the intricacies of wireless networking, from the underlying technologies to the challenges of security and the strategies for optimizing wireless performance.

Wireless Standards and Technologies

Wireless networks operate based on a variety of standards and technologies, including:

- **Wi-Fi (802.11):** The most common wireless technology, Wi-Fi operates in various frequency bands and offers different standards such as 802.11n, 802.11ac, and the latest 802.11ax (Wi-Fi 6). These standards provide varying speeds, ranges, and capabilities.
- **Bluetooth:** Used primarily for short-range connections,

Bluetooth enables devices to communicate wirelessly, often for peripheral connections like keyboards, headphones, and IoT devices.

- **Cellular Networks:** Cellular technologies like 4G LTE and 5G provide wireless data connectivity over larger areas, powering mobile devices and enabling high-speed internet access.

Wireless Security

Securing wireless networks is paramount, as they are vulnerable to eavesdropping, unauthorized access, and data breaches. Key security considerations include:

- **Encryption:** Enabling encryption protocols like WPA3 (Wi-Fi Protected Access 3) to protect data transmissions from interception.
- **Authentication:** Implementing strong authentication methods, such as using complex passwords or leveraging enterprise-level authentication mechanisms.
- **Network Segmentation:** Isolating wireless networks from wired networks using VLANs to prevent unauthorized access to sensitive resources.
- **Rogue AP Detection:** Utilizing tools to detect and mitigate rogue access points that may compromise network security.

Troubleshooting Common Wireless Issues

Wireless networks can encounter a range of issues, such as signal interference, coverage gaps, and connectivity problems. Effective troubleshooting involves:

- **Signal Analysis:** Using tools to analyze signal strength and interference sources to optimize coverage.
- **Channel Selection:** Choosing the least congested channels to minimize interference and enhance network performance.

- **Device Compatibility:** Ensuring that devices and access points are compatible with the same wireless standards and technologies.

Conclusion

Wireless networking has unleashed the power of mobility and connectivity, transforming the way we interact with technology. As you delve into the world of wireless networks in this chapter, keep in mind that while wireless offers unparalleled convenience, it also demands meticulous security measures and strategic design considerations. Whether you're configuring a home Wi-Fi network or deploying a comprehensive corporate wireless infrastructure, a solid understanding of wireless technologies and best practices will empower you to create networks that seamlessly connect individuals and devices while safeguarding data and maintaining reliability.

7
SERVER SETUP AND CONFIGURATION

Servers are the workhorses of the digital landscape, providing essential services, hosting applications, and delivering data to clients across networks. As a system administrator, understanding how to effectively set up and configure servers is fundamental to ensuring reliable and efficient operations. This chapter delves into the intricacies of server setup and configuration, from selecting hardware to installing and optimizing server operating systems.

Types of Servers and Their Roles

Servers come in various types, each designed to fulfill specific roles and functions:

- **Web Servers:** These servers host websites and web applications, delivering content to users' browsers.
- **Database Servers:** Database servers store, manage, and retrieve data for applications and services.
- **Email Servers:** Email servers handle the sending, receiving, and storage of email messages.

- **File Servers:** File servers store and manage files, allowing users to access and share documents and data.
- **Application Servers:** Application servers host and manage software applications, allowing clients to access application functionality remotely.

Server Hardware and Virtualization

Selecting appropriate server hardware is crucial for performance, scalability, and reliability. Factors to consider include CPU power, RAM, storage capacity, and redundancy features. Virtualization technologies, such as VMware and Hyper-V, enable the creation of multiple virtual machines on a single physical server. Virtualization offers benefits like resource optimization, rapid deployment, and easier management.

Server Operating System Installation and Configuration

Installing a server operating system involves booting from installation media and following prompts to select installation options, such as partitioning disks and configuring network settings. After installation, the server operating system requires configuration, including:

- **Network Settings:** Configuring IP addresses, DNS settings, and network protocols.
- **User Accounts and Permissions:** Creating user accounts, defining access permissions, and implementing security policies.
- **Services and Roles:** Installing and configuring services and roles specific to the server's function.
- **Updates and Patches:** Applying regular updates and patches to ensure security and stability.

* * *

Conclusion

Servers are the backbone of modern computing, supporting an array of critical services and applications. As you explore the intricacies of server setup and configuration in this chapter, remember that your expertise lays the foundation for seamless digital experiences. Whether you're deploying a web server to host a dynamic website or configuring a database server to store mission-critical data, mastering the art of server setup and configuration empowers you to create resilient, high-performance environments that cater to the ever-evolving demands of the digital world.

8
SECURITY AND ACCESS CONTROL

In a digital landscape brimming with data breaches and cyber threats, security is a paramount concern for system administrators. Protecting sensitive information, maintaining data integrity, and ensuring the confidentiality of user interactions are central responsibilities. This chapter delves into the intricacies of security and access control, exploring measures to safeguard systems, manage user permissions, and implement robust security policies.

User and Group Management

Effective user and group management is essential for controlling access to resources and maintaining a secure environment. Key aspects include:

- **User Accounts:** Creating and managing user accounts with strong, unique passwords and enforcing password policies.
- **Group Accounts:** Organizing users into groups to simplify permission management and ensure consistent access controls.

- **User Roles:** Assigning specific roles to users, granting appropriate permissions based on their responsibilities.

File System Permissions

File system permissions regulate access to files and directories. They are typically categorized into three levels:

- **Read:** Users can view the content of files or directories.
- **Write:** Users can modify the content of files or create new files and directories.
- **Execute:** Users can run executable files or access directories.

File permissions are defined for three user groups: the owner of the file, members of the file's group, and others. Implementing the principle of least privilege ensures that users only have the permissions necessary to perform their tasks.

Implementing Security Policies

Security policies provide guidelines and rules for ensuring the security of systems and data. These policies cover a range of areas, including password policies, access controls, data encryption, and incident response. Policies should be clearly defined, communicated to users, and regularly reviewed and updated to adapt to changing threats.

Auditing and Monitoring

Regular auditing and monitoring are crucial for detecting suspicious activities and ensuring compliance with security policies. Monitoring tools help identify unauthorized access attempts, unusual patterns, and potential breaches. Auditing logs capture events and actions taken on systems, enabling administrators to review and investigate security incidents.

Conclusion

In an era of escalating cyber threats and digital vulnerabilities, the role of system administrators in maintaining security and access control cannot be overstated. As you delve into the world of security practices and access management in this chapter, remember that your vigilance and proactive measures contribute to the integrity of systems and the protection of sensitive data. Whether you're setting up stringent access controls, configuring robust file permissions, or defining security policies, your commitment to security ensures that the digital landscape remains a safe and trustworthy environment for individuals, organizations, and societies at large.

9

BACKUP AND DISASTER RECOVERY

In the realm of system and network administration, preparing for the unexpected is not just prudent—it's essential. Data loss, hardware failures, and unforeseen disasters can disrupt operations and compromise critical information. This chapter delves into the realm of backup and disaster recovery, exploring strategies to safeguard data, ensure business continuity, and recover from unexpected setbacks.

Importance of Data Backup

Data backup is the process of creating copies of critical data to safeguard against data loss due to hardware failures, human errors, malware attacks, or natural disasters. Key aspects of data backup include:

- **Regular Backup Schedule:** Establishing a routine schedule for backups to ensure that recent data is protected.
- **Full and Incremental Backups:** Using a combination of full backups (entire data) and incremental backups (changes

since the last backup) to optimize storage and backup time.
- **Offsite Backup:** Storing backups offsite to protect against physical damage or disasters that could affect the primary location.

Backup Strategies and Solutions

Various backup strategies cater to different organizational needs:

- **Local Backups:** Storing backups on local devices or servers for quick access and recovery.
- **Remote Backups:** Utilizing cloud-based backup solutions to securely store data offsite.
- **Hybrid Backups:** Combining local and remote backups for comprehensive protection.

Disaster Recovery Planning and Testing

Disaster recovery involves preparing for and responding to major disruptions that could affect an organization's operations. Key steps include:

- **Disaster Recovery Plan:** Developing a comprehensive plan that outlines procedures, roles, and responsibilities in the event of a disaster.
- **Business Impact Analysis:** Identifying critical systems, applications, and data, and assessing the potential impact of their loss.
- **Testing and Simulation:** Regularly testing the disaster recovery plan through simulations to ensure its effectiveness and identify areas for improvement.

Conclusion

In a digital world marked by uncertainty and potential threats, the role of a system administrator extends beyond the everyday management of systems. As you delve into the realm of backup and disaster recovery in this chapter, remember that your commitment to data protection and business continuity safeguards the integrity of operations and the confidence of stakeholders. Whether you're implementing robust backup solutions, crafting comprehensive disaster recovery plans, or conducting simulated recovery exercises, your efforts play a vital role in ensuring that organizations can weather storms, emerge resilient, and continue to thrive even in the face of unforeseen challenges.

10
CLOUD COMPUTING AND VIRTUALIZATION

The digital landscape has undergone a paradigm shift with the advent of cloud computing and virtualization technologies. These innovations have redefined the way organizations manage their IT resources, offering scalability, flexibility, and cost-efficiency. In this chapter, we delve into the world of cloud computing and virtualization, exploring their benefits, challenges, and the role of system administrators in harnessing their potential.

Introduction to Cloud Computing

Cloud computing refers to the delivery of computing resources, including storage, processing power, and applications, over the internet. Cloud services are categorized into three main models:

- **Infrastructure as a Service (IaaS):** Provides virtualized computing resources, such as virtual machines and storage, allowing organizations to deploy and manage their applications.
- **Platform as a Service (PaaS):** Offers a platform and

environment for developers to build, deploy, and manage applications without worrying about infrastructure management.

- **Software as a Service (SaaS):** Delivers fully functional applications over the internet, eliminating the need for installation and maintenance.

Benefits of Cloud Computing

Cloud computing offers numerous advantages for organizations, including:

- **Scalability:** Organizations can scale resources up or down based on demand, without the need for significant infrastructure investments.
- **Cost Efficiency:** Cloud services often follow a pay-as-you-go model, eliminating the need for upfront capital expenses.
- **Flexibility:** Cloud environments allow for rapid deployment and experimentation with new applications and services.

Virtualization Technologies

Virtualization is the practice of creating virtual instances of resources, such as servers, operating systems, or storage, on a single physical machine. Key virtualization technologies include:

- **Server Virtualization:** Creating multiple virtual machines on a single physical server, allowing efficient utilization of resources.
- **Network Virtualization:** Decoupling network services from hardware, enabling greater flexibility in managing and configuring networks.
- **Storage Virtualization:** Abstracting physical storage resources to create a virtual pool of storage that can be allocated as needed.

Managing Virtual Machines in the Cloud

As a system administrator, managing virtual machines in the cloud involves tasks such as:

- **Provisioning:** Deploying and configuring virtual machines to meet specific requirements.
- **Monitoring:** Monitoring the performance and health of virtual machines to ensure optimal operations.
- **Scaling:** Scaling virtual resources up or down based on demand to optimize resource utilization.

Conclusion

Cloud computing and virtualization have transformed the landscape of IT administration, offering new avenues for efficiency, scalability, and innovation. As you explore the intricacies of cloud computing and virtualization in this chapter, remember that your role as a system administrator extends beyond physical hardware. By mastering these technologies, you empower organizations to embrace the future of computing, scale their operations seamlessly, and leverage the power of virtual resources to create resilient, adaptable, and forward-looking IT environments.

11
AUTOMATION AND SCRIPTING

In the ever-evolving world of system and network administration, the ability to automate tasks and streamline processes has become a game-changer. Automation not only enhances efficiency but also reduces the risk of human errors and frees up administrators to focus on more strategic initiatives. This chapter explores the realm of automation and scripting, from scripting languages to the deployment of configuration management tools.

Scripting Languages for Automation

Scripting languages are essential tools for automating repetitive tasks and managing system configurations. Common scripting languages include:

- **Bash:** A Unix shell and command language for automating tasks in Unix-like operating systems.
- **Python:** A versatile and widely-used scripting language known for its simplicity and readability.
- **PowerShell:** A scripting language designed for Windows

environments, used for automating administrative tasks.

Benefits of Automation

Automation offers numerous advantages for system administrators:

- **Time Savings:** Automating routine tasks frees up time for administrators to focus on more complex and strategic activities.
- **Consistency:** Automated processes are executed consistently, reducing the risk of human errors.
- **Scalability:** Automated processes can be easily scaled to accommodate growing workloads.
- **Efficiency:** Automation allows administrators to accomplish tasks faster, even in complex environments.

Configuration Management Tools

Configuration management tools help administrators manage and automate system configurations across multiple servers. Popular tools include:

- **Puppet:** A configuration management tool that defines system configurations as code and ensures consistency across systems.
- **Chef:** A platform for automating infrastructure configuration and software deployment.
- **Ansible:** An open-source automation tool that focuses on task automation, requiring minimal setup.
- **SaltStack:** A configuration management and orchestration tool that uses a client-server architecture.

Deploying Automation Solutions

Implementing automation solutions involves steps such as:

- **Identifying Targets:** Determining which tasks or processes can benefit from automation.
- **Scripting or Tool Selection:** Choosing the appropriate

scripting language or configuration management tool for the task.

- **Creating Scripts or Playbooks:** Developing scripts or playbooks that define the desired automated actions.
- **Testing:** Thoroughly testing automation scripts or configurations in a controlled environment.
- **Deployment:** Deploying the automation solution to the target systems or environment.

Conclusion

In the dynamic world of system and network administration, automation and scripting have emerged as indispensable skills. As you delve into the realm of automation in this chapter, remember that mastering these tools empowers you to transform manual tasks into efficient, repeatable processes. Whether you're creating scripts to streamline routine tasks, implementing configuration management solutions, or orchestrating complex workflows, your ability to harness the power of automation enables you to navigate the complexities of modern IT administration with agility, precision, and innovation.

12
MONITORING AND PERFORMANCE OPTIMIZATION

In the ever-evolving landscape of system and network administration, monitoring and optimizing the performance of IT environments stand as critical tasks. The ability to proactively detect issues, ensure optimal resource utilization, and fine-tune systems is essential for maintaining efficient operations. This chapter delves into the world of monitoring, performance optimization, and the tools that empower administrators to keep systems running at their best.

Importance of Monitoring

Monitoring involves continuously tracking system metrics, resource usage, and performance indicators to ensure the health and availability of IT resources. Key aspects of monitoring include:

- **Real-time Visibility:** Providing real-time insights into system performance and resource utilization.

- **Early Detection:** Identifying and addressing issues before they escalate and impact users.
- **Data Analysis:** Collecting data to analyze trends and make informed decisions for optimization.

Key Performance Indicators (KPIs)

KPIs provide a quantitative measure of system performance. Examples include:

- **Response Time:** Measuring the time it takes for a system to respond to user requests.
- **Throughput:** Measuring the rate at which data is transferred between components.
- **Resource Utilization:** Monitoring CPU, memory, disk, and network usage to ensure efficient resource allocation.

Monitoring Tools and Solutions

Monitoring tools provide insights into system health and performance. Examples of monitoring tools include:

- **Nagios:** An open-source tool that monitors hosts, services, and network devices.
- **Zabbix:** A versatile monitoring solution that offers real-time monitoring, alerting, and visualization.
- **Prometheus:** An open-source monitoring and alerting toolkit with a focus on time series data.

Performance Optimization Strategies

Performance optimization involves improving system speed, responsiveness, and resource utilization. Strategies include:

- **Load Balancing:** Distributing network or application traffic across multiple servers to prevent overload.
- **Caching:** Storing frequently accessed data in memory to reduce the need to fetch it from slower storage.
- **Resource Tuning:** Adjusting system parameters to optimize

resource allocation and utilization.
- **Database Optimization:** Indexing databases, optimizing queries, and managing database connections to improve performance.

Conclusion

In the dynamic realm of system and network administration, monitoring and performance optimization are the bedrock of efficient operations. As you delve into the intricacies of monitoring and optimization in this chapter, remember that your vigilance and proactive measures contribute to the resilience, responsiveness, and reliability of IT environments. Whether you're deploying monitoring tools to detect anomalies, fine-tuning system parameters, or optimizing database performance, your commitment to monitoring and optimization ensures that organizations can deliver seamless user experiences, achieve peak operational efficiency, and navigate the complexities of technology with confidence and success.

13
CONTINUOUS LEARNING AND PROFESSIONAL GROWTH

In the ever-evolving landscape of system and network administration, staying current with the latest technologies, trends, and best practices is not only essential—it's a mindset that sets exceptional administrators apart. Continuous learning and professional growth are the keys to remaining relevant, adaptable, and successful in the dynamic world of IT administration. This chapter delves into the importance of lifelong learning, strategies for staying informed, and the path to becoming a well-rounded and proficient system and network administrator.

The Need for Continuous Learning

Technology evolves at a rapid pace, and system administrators must keep pace to remain effective. Continuous learning offers numerous benefits:

- **Adaptability:** Staying updated allows administrators to adapt to new tools and practices seamlessly.
- **Innovation:** Learning about emerging technologies fosters

innovation and creative problem-solving.

- **Career Growth:** Continuous learning enhances skills, making administrators more valuable to organizations.

Staying Informed and Current

Staying informed involves actively seeking out relevant information and resources:

- **Online Communities:** Participating in online forums, discussion boards, and social media groups dedicated to system and network administration.
- **Blogs and Websites:** Following industry blogs, news websites, and authoritative sources for updates and insights.
- **Professional Organizations:** Joining professional organizations and attending conferences or webinars to connect with peers and gain insights.

Skill Diversification

Becoming a proficient system and network administrator involves developing a broad range of skills:

- **Technical Skills:** Mastering operating systems, networking protocols, scripting languages, and cloud technologies.
- **Soft Skills:** Developing communication, problem-solving, and collaboration skills to interact effectively with colleagues and stakeholders.
- **Security Expertise:** Keeping up with evolving cybersecurity threats and countermeasures to protect digital assets.

Certifications and Training

Certifications validate skills and expertise, enhancing career prospects:

- **CompTIA A+:** Entry-level certification covering fundamental IT skills and knowledge.

- **Cisco CCNA:** Certifying proficiency in networking fundamentals and Cisco devices.
- **Microsoft MCSE:** Demonstrating expertise in Microsoft server technologies and solutions.
- **Certified Information Systems Security Professional (CISSP):** Recognizing expertise in cybersecurity and information security management.

Conclusion

In the dynamic realm of system and network administration, the journey doesn't end with mastering tools and techniques—it's a continuous voyage of growth, adaptation, and innovation. As you explore the world of continuous learning and professional growth in this chapter, remember that your commitment to staying informed and evolving your skill set empowers you to navigate the ever-changing IT landscape with confidence and expertise. Whether you're embracing new technologies, honing soft skills, pursuing certifications, or networking with peers, your dedication to lifelong learning ensures that you're equipped to face challenges, seize opportunities, and thrive in the exciting journey of system and network administration.

14

ETHICS AND PROFESSIONALISM IN SYSTEM AND NETWORK ADMINISTRATION

In the world of system and network administration, technical expertise is only one facet of success. Ethical conduct and professionalism are equally essential, shaping the reputation of administrators and the organizations they serve. This chapter delves into the importance of ethics and professionalism in the field, exploring the principles that guide administrators' behavior, interactions, and responsibilities.

Ethical Principles in System Administration

Ethical considerations are integral to the decision-making process of system administrators:

- **Integrity:** Upholding honesty, transparency, and accuracy in all actions and communications.
- **Confidentiality:** Safeguarding sensitive information and respecting user privacy.

- **Accountability:** Taking responsibility for actions, decisions, and the consequences that arise from them.
- **Fairness:** Treating all users, colleagues, and stakeholders equitably and impartially.

Professionalism in Interactions

Professionalism extends to interactions within and outside the organization:

- **Communication:** Effective and respectful communication with colleagues, users, and stakeholders.
- **Collaboration:** Fostering teamwork, sharing knowledge, and valuing diverse perspectives.
- **Conflict Resolution:** Addressing conflicts constructively and seeking resolutions that benefit all parties.

Balancing Organizational and User Needs

System administrators often find themselves at the intersection of organizational goals and user needs:

- **User-Centric Approach:** Prioritizing user experience, addressing concerns, and providing assistance promptly.
- **Organizational Alignment:** Aligning technical decisions with organizational objectives and strategies.

Ethical Considerations in Security and Data Privacy

In an era marked by data breaches and privacy concerns, ethical choices are paramount:

- **Security Practices:** Implementing robust security measures to protect systems, data, and user information.
- **Data Privacy:** Adhering to data protection regulations and ensuring user consent for data collection and processing.

Continuing Education and Ethical Reflection

Ethics and professionalism require ongoing reflection and education:

- **Continuous Learning:** Staying informed about emerging ethical challenges and evolving standards.
- **Scenario Analysis:** Evaluating potential ethical dilemmas in advance and determining the best course of action.

Conclusion

In the realm of system and network administration, technical competence goes hand in hand with ethical behavior and professionalism. As you explore the importance of ethics and professionalism in this chapter, remember that your actions and decisions as an administrator influence the trust users place in your expertise and the organization's commitment to ethical conduct. By embracing ethical principles, fostering professionalism in interactions, and prioritizing the needs of users and organizations, you contribute to a trustworthy, respectful, and effective environment that benefits not only your career but the entire digital community.

15

FUTURE TRENDS AND EMERGING TECHNOLOGIES

In the dynamic landscape of system and network administration, staying attuned to emerging trends and technologies is vital for remaining ahead of the curve. The field is continually evolving, driven by technological advancements that shape the way systems are managed and networks are operated. This chapter explores the future trends and emerging technologies that administrators should be aware of, offering insights into the direction of the field and the skills needed to stay relevant.

Edge Computing and Internet of Things (IoT)

Edge computing involves processing data closer to its source, reducing latency and improving real-time decision-making. As IoT devices proliferate, administrators must adapt to managing decentralized computing environments and ensuring data security.

5G Networks

The rollout of 5G networks promises significantly faster data speeds and lower latency. Administrators will need to optimize network infrastructure to accommodate the increased traffic and ensure seamless connectivity.

Artificial Intelligence (AI) and Machine Learning (ML)

AI and ML are transforming IT operations, enabling predictive analysis, automation, and anomaly detection. Administrators will need to understand how to leverage these technologies to streamline processes and enhance system reliability.

Serverless Computing

Serverless computing abstracts server management, allowing developers to focus solely on writing code. Administrators will need to adapt to this paradigm shift and ensure seamless integration between serverless platforms and traditional infrastructure.

Containers and Microservices

Containers and microservices offer greater scalability and agility in application deployment. Administrators must master container orchestration tools like Kubernetes to manage these distributed applications effectively.

Cybersecurity and Privacy

As technology evolves, so do cyber threats. Administrators will need to stay updated on the latest cybersecurity measures, encryption technologies, and data privacy regulations to safeguard digital assets effectively.

Hybrid Cloud Environments

Hybrid cloud environments, combining public and private clouds, offer flexibility and scalability. Administrators will need to manage and optimize resources across these diverse platforms.

Quantum Computing

While still in its infancy, quantum computing has the potential to revolutionize computing power. Administrators should stay informed about its progress and explore how it might impact IT operations.

Skills for the Future

As the landscape evolves, administrators must cultivate a diverse skill set:

- **Adaptability:** Being open to change and willing to learn new

technologies as they emerge.
- **Strategic Thinking:** Understanding how emerging trends align with organizational goals.
- **Interdisciplinary Knowledge:** Embracing cross-disciplinary knowledge in areas like cybersecurity, data science, and machine learning.

Conclusion

In the realm of system and network administration, the future promises exciting advancements and transformative changes. As you explore the future trends and emerging technologies in this chapter, remember that your willingness to embrace change, learn new skills, and adapt to evolving landscapes is key to your success as a professional. By staying informed about the latest developments and continuously expanding your knowledge, you position yourself as a valuable asset in the dynamic world of IT administration, ready to navigate new challenges and seize emerging opportunities with confidence and expertise.

16

THE EVOLVING ROLE OF SYSTEM AND NETWORK ADMINISTRATORS

The role of system and network administrators has undergone a remarkable evolution in parallel with technological advancements and changing business landscapes. From managing hardware to orchestrating complex digital ecosystems, administrators have become pivotal players in driving innovation and ensuring seamless operations. This chapter explores the evolving nature of the role, the skills required, and the future expectations for system and network administrators.

From Technicians to Strategists

Traditionally, administrators were seen as technicians responsible for maintaining hardware and troubleshooting issues. Today, they have evolved into strategic thinkers and technology enablers who contribute to organizational growth.

Emphasis on Automation

Automation has become a cornerstone of modern administration. Administrators are no longer focused solely on manual tasks but are empowered to script, automate, and orchestrate complex processes, freeing up time for higher-level tasks.

DevOps and Collaboration

The rise of DevOps culture emphasizes collaboration between development and operations teams. Administrators are expected to work seamlessly with developers, fostering a culture of continuous integration and deployment.

Security and Compliance

In an era marked by cybersecurity threats and data privacy concerns, administrators play a crucial role in safeguarding systems and ensuring compliance with regulations. Security is no longer an afterthought but an integral part of the role.

Hybrid and Cloud Environments

The shift to hybrid and cloud environments demands a new set of skills. Administrators must navigate the complexities of managing both on-premises infrastructure and cloud services, ensuring seamless integration and resource optimization.

User-Centric Approach

Administrators are increasingly adopting a user-centric approach, focusing on delivering exceptional user experiences. This involves understanding user needs, providing efficient support, and optimizing systems for user satisfaction.

Skills Beyond Technical Proficiency

While technical skills remain crucial, administrators are expected to possess a diverse skill set:

- **Soft Skills:** Effective communication, problem-solving, and collaboration skills are essential for interactions with colleagues, users, and stakeholders.
- **Adaptability:** Rapid technological changes require administrators to be quick learners and adaptable to new tools and practices.
- **Business Acumen:** Understanding how technology aligns with business goals and contributes to organizational success.

Continuous Learning and Professional Growth

As the role continues to evolve, administrators must embrace continuous learning:

- **Stay Informed:** Keeping up with emerging technologies, trends, and best practices is essential.
- **Certifications:** Pursuing relevant certifications validates expertise and enhances career prospects.
- **Networking:** Building professional connections within the

industry fosters learning and collaboration.

Conclusion

The role of a system and network administrator is no longer confined to managing hardware and troubleshooting issues. As you explore the evolving nature of the role in this chapter, remember that your adaptability, strategic thinking, and commitment to continuous learning define your success. By embracing new technologies, fostering collaboration, prioritizing security and user satisfaction, and staying ahead of industry trends, you position yourself as a pivotal player in the ever-changing landscape of system and network administration. Your ability to navigate this evolution with agility and expertise empowers you to not only manage systems but also shape the technological future of your organization.

17
Building a Successful Career in System and Network Administration

A successful career in system and network administration requires more than technical expertise—it demands a combination of skills, strategies, and a proactive mindset. As the digital landscape evolves, so do the opportunities and challenges for administrators. This chapter explores the essential elements for building a thriving and fulfilling career in system and network administration.

Defining Your Career Path

Start by defining your career goals and aspirations:

- **Specialization:** Identify areas of interest, such as security, cloud computing, or network architecture, to specialize in.
- **Long-Term Goals:** Outline where you see yourself in five, ten, or twenty years, and plan your career trajectory accordingly.

* * *

Continuous Learning and Skill Enhancement

Technology evolves rapidly, making continuous learning a cornerstone of a successful career:

- **Stay Updated:** Keep abreast of industry trends, emerging technologies, and best practices.
- **Skill Diversification:** Develop a broad skill set that encompasses both technical and soft skills.
- **Certifications:** Pursue relevant certifications to validate your expertise and enhance your credibility.

Networking and Building Relationships

Networking is essential for career growth:

- **Professional Organizations:** Join industry associations, attend conferences, and engage in online forums to connect with peers.
- **Mentorship:** Seek guidance from experienced professionals who can offer insights and advice.
- **Collaboration:** Collaborate with colleagues, both within and outside your organization, to exchange knowledge and experiences.

Problem-Solving and Critical Thinking

Problem-solving skills are integral to an administrator's role:

- **Analytical Thinking:** Approach challenges with a systematic and analytical mindset to identify root causes.
- **Creative Solutions:** Think outside the box and consider innovative solutions to complex issues.

Communication and Soft Skills

Effective communication and interpersonal skills are vital:

- **Clear Communication:** Communicate technical information concisely and clearly to both technical and non-technical audiences.
- **Conflict Resolution:** Address conflicts professionally and work towards amicable resolutions.

Adaptability and Resilience

The IT landscape is ever-changing, demanding adaptability and resilience:

- **Embrace Change:** Embrace new technologies and methodologies with an open mind.
- **Resilience:** Bounce back from setbacks and challenges with determination and a positive attitude.

Work-Life Balance and Well-Being

A successful career is balanced by personal well-being:

- **Time Management:** Prioritize tasks and set boundaries to maintain a healthy work-life balance.
- **Continuous Learning:** Pursue personal hobbies and interests outside of work to nurture your personal growth.

Conclusion

Building a successful career in system and network administration requires a multifaceted approach that encompasses technical skills, interpersonal abilities, and personal well-being. As you explore the elements of a successful career in this chapter, remember that your journey is unique, and your commitment to continuous learning, collaboration, and personal growth paves the way for a fulfilling and impactful career. By combining technical expertise with soft skills, staying adaptable and resilient, and nurturing professional relationships, you position yourself as a valued and sought-after professional in the ever-evolving field of system and network administration.

18

Navigating Challenges in System and Network Administration

In the intricate landscape of system and network administration, challenges are an inevitable part of the journey. Whether technical, organizational, or interpersonal, these challenges provide opportunities for growth and innovation. This chapter explores the common challenges administrators may face and offers strategies to navigate them effectively, ensuring the resilience and success of IT operations.

Technical Challenges

1. **Hardware Failures:** Equipment failures can disrupt operations. Implement redundancy and backup strategies to minimize downtime.

2. **Software Glitches:** Bugs, software conflicts, and compatibility issues can impact system stability. Thorough testing and updates are essential.

3. **Security Threats:** Cyberattacks, malware, and data breaches are constant threats. Maintain robust security measures, regular patching, and employee training.

4. **Scalability:** Adapting to growth and increased demands requires planning and scalability measures.

Operational Challenges

1. **Resource Allocation:** Efficiently allocating and managing resources is essential for performance. Regularly assess resource utilization and optimize as needed.

2. **Downtime and Maintenance:** Scheduled downtime for maintenance can impact operations. Plan and communicate downtime effectively to minimize disruption.

3. **Backup and Recovery:** Ensuring data backup and disaster recovery plans work seamlessly is crucial for business continuity.

4. **Compliance and Regulations:** Staying compliant with industry regulations and data protection laws can be complex. Regular audits and staying informed are key.

Interpersonal Challenges

1. **Communication Issues:** Miscommunication between technical and non-technical teams can lead to misunderstandings. Foster clear communication channels.

2. **Conflict Resolution:** Conflicts can arise within teams or with users. Address conflicts constructively and seek resolutions that benefit all parties.

3. **User Expectations:** Users may have high expectations for

system performance. Educate users about realistic expectations and offer clear support channels.

4. **Balancing Workload:** Balancing daily tasks with unexpected challenges can be overwhelming. Prioritize tasks and seek assistance when needed.

Adapting to Change Challenges

1. **Rapid Technological Changes:** Staying current with evolving technologies can be challenging. Dedicate time to continuous learning and experimentation.

2. **Resistance to Change:** Team members or stakeholders may resist adopting new tools or practices. Communicate the benefits and involve them in the process.

3. **Cultural Shifts:** Organizational shifts in culture or strategies can impact IT operations. Embrace change and align IT goals with organizational objectives.

4. **Budget Constraints:** Limited budgets may hinder investment in necessary resources. Advocate for the importance of IT investments and demonstrate their value.

Conclusion

Challenges in system and network administration are not roadblocks but stepping stones for growth and improvement. As you explore the strategies to navigate challenges in this chapter, remember that your ability to adapt, problem-solve, and collaborate contributes to the resilience and success of IT operations. By approaching challenges with a proactive mindset, leveraging technical expertise, and fostering effective communication, you empower yourself to transform hurdles into opportunities for innovation, learning, and ultimately, the advancement of your career and the organizations you serve.

19
CONCLUSION

Conclusion: Navigating the Digital Frontier - A Guide to System and Network Administration

In the ever-changing landscape of technology, the role of system and network administrators stands as a beacon of stability, guiding organizations through the complexities of digital operations. As we conclude this comprehensive guide to system and network administration, it's clear that this discipline is not just about managing servers and networks; it's about shaping the future of technology, safeguarding data, and enabling innovation.

From the foundational understanding of system architectures and operating systems to the intricate realm of security, automation, and emerging technologies, each chapter has unveiled a facet of the administrator's multifaceted role. Through the pages of this book, we've delved into the intricacies of networking protocols, the nuances of access control, the art of scripting, and the wisdom of continuous learning.

We've explored the importance of ethics, professionalism, and collaboration in the digital realm, recognizing that success is built on not only technical prowess but also on the ability to communicate, adapt, and work harmoniously with diverse teams.

As you embark on your journey as a system and network administrator, remember that your role is not merely to manage technology, but to shape it. You are the architects of digital landscapes, the defenders of data integrity, and the enablers of seamless user experiences. Your dedication to staying informed, embracing change, and fostering innovation positions you at the forefront of technological advancement.

The road ahead may be challenging, but armed with the knowledge, insights, and strategies laid out in this guide, you are equipped to conquer any obstacle and seize countless opportunities. With each system you optimize, each network you secure, and each challenge you overcome, you contribute to the evolution of technology and the success of the organizations you serve.

As you embark on this exhilarating journey, may this guide serve as your compass, guiding you through the intricate terrain of system and network administration. Embrace the challenges, celebrate the victories, and remember that your role transcends technology—it's about empowering organizations, shaping the digital landscape, and leaving an indelible mark on the world of technology.

Access Control: The practice of regulating and restricting access to computer systems, networks, and resources based on user roles and permissions.

Automation: The use of scripts, tools, or software to automate repetitive tasks and processes, reducing manual intervention and improving efficiency.

Backup: The process of creating copies of data or system configurations to protect against data loss due to hardware failures, human errors, or disasters.

Cloud Computing: The delivery of computing resources, such as storage, processing power, and applications, over the internet on a pay-as-you-go basis.

Configuration Management: The practice of tracking and managing changes to software, hardware, and network configurations to ensure consistency and compliance.

DNS (Domain Name System): A system that translates human-readable domain names into IP addresses, allowing users to access websites using familiar names.

Firewall: A security system that controls and monitors incoming and outgoing network traffic to prevent unauthorized access and potential threats.

IPv4 and IPv6: Internet Protocol versions 4 and 6, responsible for assigning unique IP addresses to devices on a network, enabling communication over the internet.

Load Balancing: The distribution of network or application traffic across multiple servers to ensure optimal resource utilization and prevent server overload.

Network Protocol: A set of rules and conventions that govern communication between devices on a network, ensuring data transmission accuracy.

Operating System: Software that manages hardware resources, provides user interfaces, and runs applications on a computer or server.

Patch Management: The process of applying software updates, or patches, to systems and applications to fix vulnerabilities and improve security.

Root User: The superuser or administrator account in Unix-like operating systems with full control over the system.

Scripting Language: A programming language used to write scripts that automate tasks or perform specific functions, often used in system administration.

Security Policy: A set of guidelines and rules that define how an organization protects its systems, data, and resources from security threats.

Server: A computer or software that provides services, resources, or data to other computers or clients on a network.

SSH (Secure Shell): A cryptographic network protocol used to securely access and manage remote servers and devices over an unsecured network.

Syslog: A standard protocol used for sending and receiving log and event messages in a network.

Virtualization: The practice of creating virtual instances of hardware, software, or networks on a single physical machine to optimize resource utilization.

VPN (Virtual Private Network): A secure connection that encrypts internet traffic, providing privacy and anonymity while accessing the internet.

Wireless Network: A network that uses radio waves to connect devices, enabling wireless communication and internet access.

This glossary provides brief explanations of key terms encountered in the field of system and network administration. Familiarity with these terms will enhance your understanding of the concepts discussed throughout the book.

Expanding your knowledge and staying informed in the field of system and network administration requires ongoing learning and exploration. Here are some additional resources and references that can provide valuable insights, tutorials, and further information:

Books:

1. Limoncelli, T. A., Hogan, C., & Chalup, S. R. (2021). "The Practice of System and Network Administration: Volume 1 - DevOps and other Best Practices for Enterprise IT" (3rd Edition). Pearson.

2. Hunt, C., & Thompson, M. (2021). "The Pragmatic Programmer: Your Journey to Mastery." Addison-Wesley Professional.

3. Burgess, M., Nance, J., & Pletcher, W. (2020). "Linux Server Security: Hack and Defend." Wiley.

Online Resources:

1. **Stack Overflow:** An online community where you can ask and answer technical questions related to system administration and programming.

2. **GitHub:** Explore repositories and projects related to system administration, scripts, and automation.

3. **Reddit Communities:** Subreddits like r/sysadmin and r/networking offer discussions, news, and insights from fellow professionals.

4. **Server Fault:** A community-driven Q&A site for system administrators and IT professionals to seek advice and share knowledge.

5. **Linux Documentation Project:** A valuable resource for Linux system administration guides, how-tos, and tutorials.

Online Courses and Platforms:

1. **Coursera:** Offers courses on networking, security, Linux administration, and more from universities and institutions worldwide.

2. **edX:** Provides courses from universities and institutions on topics like cybersecurity, cloud computing, and IT management.

3. **Udemy:** Offers a variety of courses on system administration, scripting, and other IT-related topics.

4. **LinkedIn Learning:** Provides a range of video courses on system administration, cybersecurity, and IT skills.

Industry Blogs and News:

1. **Ars Technica:** Offers news, reviews, and analysis on technology, security, and IT trends.

2. **Dark Reading:** Focuses on cybersecurity news, insights, and analysis for IT professionals.

3. **The Register:** Provides news, reviews, and insights on technology, networking, and IT.

4. **ZDNet:** Offers technology news, analysis, and commentary on various IT topics.

These additional resources and references can be valuable tools to enhance your learning, stay updated on industry trends, and expand your expertise in the dynamic field of system and network administration.

Made in United States
North Haven, CT
09 October 2023

42554375R00043